Toulouse
Travel Guide

Quick Trips Series

Table of Contents

Toulouse

Toulouse is a city in the southwest of France inland

between the Atlantic Ocean and the Mediterranean Sea.

Toulouse is an important part of the French economy and

is a major center for the aviation and space industry with

the head offices of Airbus, European Aeronautic Defence

and Space Company (EADS), and the Galileo Navigation

Satellite System.

TOULOUSE TRAVEL GUIDE

Toulouse (pronounced tu-luz) has a rich history in architecture and education. The city has modernized in the last 3 decades under the leadership of the Baudis – the father-son duo who held the seat of Mayor from 1983 to 2001. Today Toulouse is not only a major corporate zone, but also a favorite tourist destination.

The Pink City in daytime and the City of Lights at night, Toulouse grew up in the banks of the river Garonne. Earliest records trace to Roman settlements in that area. In fact the brick architecture that is so predominant in the city is a reflection of the Roman past. The brick buildings look pinkish in the sunlight, thus giving the city its nickname the Ville Rose – Pink City.

TOULOUSE TRAVEL GUIDE

In fact, if one looks at a satellite picture of Toulouse in daytime, it looks like a pink patch on the banks of the Garonne. The city is also called the City of Lights because of the innumerable illuminated sights at night.

The city, fourth largest in France, after Paris, Lyon, and Marseille, in terms of population, is rich in Gothic, Roman, and Renaissance architecture. One can wander along its narrow Romanesque lanes of the old town or take a boat ride (€ 8) along the river to enjoy the beauty of the city that dates back to the second century AD.

The earliest settlements in the city were by the Celts and the Romans, almost 2 thousand years ago. It was made a royal city in the thirteenth century triggering a growth in art and education. After suffering a plague, war, and famine in the 14th century, the city's fortune turned in the 15th

century through commerce.

Although it did not last long, Toulouse started modernizing

during the late 19th century. With major immigration in the

20th century, trade and commerce grew, attracting major

business houses to invest in Toulouse. Today, Toulouse

is the capital of the Midi-Pyrenees region of France and is

not only a stop for the business traveler, but an equally

important destination for students as well as tourists.

🌏 Customs & Culture

Toulouse is dotted with architecture from the medieval

European period. A casual stroll by foot at the old town

with an occasional café break is ideal for a lazy afternoon.

Most of the city attractions are on the right bank of the

Garonne. The city has 120,000 students (the 2nd largest in France after Paris) and has a strong alternative music and arts scene. There are spots spread across town that hold regular events like the Mix'Art Myrys - http://mixart-myrys.org/ -, La Dynamo - http://www.ladynamo-toulouse.com/, and the L'Usine - http://www.lusine.net/.

Every February Toulouse hosts the Festival de la Violette or the Festival of the Violets – the emblematic flower of the city. For a month the city is transformed to the City of Violets! Summer in Toulouse is a time for music festivals all over the city. The Toulouse International Art Festival (previously called the Spring in September Festival), Rio Loco Festival, Les Siestes Electroniques, and the Tangopostale offer a variety of music and dance from all corners of the earth.

TOULOUSE TRAVEL GUIDE

One of the major events in the winter months is the Toulouse les Orgues - http://www.toulouse-les-orgues.org/ - in October. Toulouse is known for its variety of organs – 9 of the 30 organs in the city are historical monuments. This event highlights Toulouse's favorite instrument.

One can also catch a sporting event in the city. Although Toulouse has a soccer team playing in the French Ligue 1, it is the rugby team, Stade Toulosain that has made the city proud time and again. It has won the coveted Heineken Cup 4 times since 1996. The city has some world-class venues and has hosted world cup games in soccer and rugby.

The tourist pass of Toulouse known as the 'Pass tourisme' gives discounts on entry to a number of tourist attractions. They can be bought at tourist offices and come in 3 options – 24 hr (€ 18), 36 hr (€ 25) and 72 hr (€ 32)

Geography

Toulouse is 580km from Paris and 321km from Marseilles. Barcelona, though, is closer to this French city at a distance of only 254km. There are regular flight and bus services connecting Toulouse to other French and European cities.

Bus service by Alsa connects Toulouse directly with other countries like Italy, Spain, Portugal, and Switzerland. Eurolines also operates through Toulouse and connects it with other major and smaller French and European cities. The bus station near the main railway station is Gare Routiere.

TOULOUSE TRAVEL GUIDE

Toulouse's main airport, the Blagnac Airport (IATA: TLS), is 8km from the city and is a 30 minute ride in the airport shuttle bus, costing € 5. The shuttle operates at a frequency of 20 minutes and connects both the airport and the main railway station – Gare Matabiau. It is also connected with the city bus service through bus line 66. The Blagnac Airport connects Toulouse with 30 countries worldwide and there are nearly 30 airlines operating from the city.

The Gare Matibiau is the main train station of Toulouse and is located at the city centre. The train schedules can be checked at the SNCF website or at the stations itself. One can buy tickets (billets in French) from the counter or the vending machines but it must be validated before a journey. Cheap tickets can be bought online through the

TOULOUSE TRAVEL GUIDE

iDTGV website. One needs to check the destination of the car/coach before boarding as trains are often split and cars moved to another train.

For visitors it is a good idea to buy a 24-hr (€ 18), 48-hr (€ 25) or a 72-hr (€ 32) pass. The pass allows unlimited metro, bus, and airport shuttle, as well as entry to some of the tourist sites during the valid period.

Once in the city, one can use the bus, metro, tram, and cab service to move around.

TISSEO/SEMVAT operates the public bus lines in the city. Zones are color-coded denoting where a certain bus will make stops. Each ticket cost € 1.60 and needs to be validated before a journey. Unlike many European cities, buses need to be flagged down to stop, by simply raising an arm. Buses usually ply up to 10:00pm. There is a free green shuttle/bus that circles the city centre on weekdays.

The Toulouse Metro operates from 5:15am till midnight (till 1am on Fridays and Saturdays) and criss-crosses the city through Lines A, and B with the driverless trains. A metro or a bus system ticket allows free parking at some of the stations like Arenes and Jolimont.

There is a single Tram Line T1 from Toulouse to Beauzelle. It passes through Blagnac.

Night services are available on certain lines. Schedules and details can be checked at http://www.tisseo.fr/en/getting-around .

Taxis are available throughout the city with many being parked at popular tourist sites. There are many taxi services like Capitol taxis, Taxi Aeroport, Taxi Radio Toulosain. A taxi ride from the city centre to the airport costs around €20-25. A separate fee is charged for luggage.

Bicycles can be rented from the VeloToulouse bike rental stations for as low as € 1.20 for 30 minutes. Rentals range from € 5.00 – 35.00 for the whole day depending upon the type and quality of the bicycle. The Canal du Midi has a beautiful shaded bicycle path along its banks.

🌐 Weather & Best Time to Visit

Toulouse is a landlocked city beside the Pyrenees Mountains. Almost equidistant from the Atlantic Ocean and the Mediterranean Sea, it has a temperate climate with mildly hot summers and near freezing winters. The summer temperatures rise to around 28 degrees Celsius in July and August; the winter months of December, January, and February see the temperature fall to around 3 – 4 degrees Celsius. There is precipitation all round the year. Toulouse, on an average, receives between 45mm to 55mm of precipitation every month.

Although some of the summer days are hot and humid and there is the occasional snowfall in winter, the mild weather of Toulouse makes it accessible all the year round. The spring and autumn months are mostly sunny with winds. It is suggested to dress in layers during the spring and autumn as the mornings are cold, afternoons warm, and evenings are again cold.

July and August have been the traditional holiday months for the French. One can expect a huge rush and rise in the tourist population during these months. Holiday tip: It is best to avoid traveling on July 1st and 15th, and August 1st, 15th, 31st, because the French locals, depending on their schedule, take month long holidays in July or August, or from mid-July to mid-August.

Sights & Activities: What to See & Do

 **Place du Capitole**

31000 Toulouse

Location: Centre / Capitole

Tel: 0561 223412

TOULOUSE TRAVEL GUIDE

At the heart of the old city centre is the prime attraction of Toulouse, the Place du Capitole. It is a complex of buildings and a huge square which has been made a pedestrian zone.

It was back in 1190 when the governing magistrates – the capitoulus – decided to build a building for public administration and a seat for the government – the Capitole de Toulouse. Eight magnificent columns paying homage to the 8 capitoulus can be seen till today. Some changes were made in 1750 and the present structure that we see, although much different from the original building, retains some of the design from 1750.

The neoclassical pink brick façade is one such feature from 1750 that still mesmerizes the visitors. The original building had a donjon – a keep (like a dungeon) – upon which a bell tower was built in 1873. The massive courtyard, one of the few structures to have survived from the medieval period has been a witness to history, the most famous being the decapitation of the Henry II Duke of Montmorency.

The year 1995 saw another major round of redesigning of the square. Along with the grand municipal buildings and the City Hall, the square now houses the Theatre du Capitole and the Farnese gallery (Rome) inspired Salle des Illustres. The Salle des Illustres is the home to some magnificent 19th century art.

The first Sunday of each month is the 'day without automobiles' at the square and that is the day to visit the Capitole. The historical Jean-Paul Laurens room, the Hall of Distinguished Henri Martin, and the Paul Gervais room are opened to the public on this day.

Today it is a large cobbled area with beautiful colonnades. The square is filled with shops and eateries. One can find traditional food items being sold as well fast food joints. The City Hall is a favorite for weddings and although entry is free for visitors, it is restricted when weddings are on.

There is free entry. It is open from 8:30am to 7:00 pm from Mon – Sat, and from 10:00am to 7:00pm on Sundays and holidays. It is closed on December 25th and January 1st.

Basilica St Sernin

Place St Sernin

31000 Toulouse

TOULOUSE TRAVEL GUIDE

Location: Centre

Tel: Basilica: 0561 217018; Archdiocese: 0561 14870;

Presbytery: 0561 218045

www.basilique-st-sernin-toulouse.fr

This 12th century Romaesque masterpiece is a UNESCO World Heritage Site and is on the northern edge of the Old Quarter of Toulouse. Construction of the original church, which was an abbey church for the Abbey of St Sernin, started around the 4th century.

There are no clear records of the original construction and the dates. In 1096 the Pope Urban II dedicated an altar confirming that construction must have started before that date. 1096 is often taken as the date of consecration of the church.

TOULOUSE TRAVEL GUIDE

Although there are no clear records of the construction, it seems that the construction was done from east to west over a period of a few hundred years, with a number of interruptions. This is because of the fact that the east walls have a predominance of stone and the western parts are more brick layered, as was with most buildings built during the Roman influence in the later centuries.

The basilica has an octagonal 5 tier tower and is in the shape of a crucifix. It is the largest church in Toulouse standing 115m in length and dominates the city skyline. An interesting feature of the church is that is has radiating chapels to display important relics. An ambulatory was built to view the treasure trove without disturbing mass. This made the basilica more of a pilgrimage church – a church that was built to host pilgrims. The church still welcomes pilgrims of St Jacques de Compostella from April 1st to October 31st every year.

This pilgrimage church has a beautiful canopy of gilded wood and marble in the interiors. The Romanesque arches lead to nine chapels. The two doorways have exquisite carvings above the entrance. The doorways are named after a nearby vault that contains the remains of 4 counts of Toulouse. Inside, the crypt has the remains of St Saturnine or St Sernin – the first bishop of Toulouse. It is also the resting place of many other saints including St Honoratus.

One of the highlights of the church is the grand Cavaille-Coll organ. This 3 manual, 32 feet organ was built in 1888 and is regarded a masterpiece of French organ building.

Admission is free.

The basilica is open from 8:30am – 6:00pm from Monday to Saturday, and till 7:00pm on Sunday. Weekday entrance is extended by an hour from Jun – Sep. The crypt and ambulatory are open from 10:00am – 12noon, and 2:00pm – 5:30pm from Monday to Saturday and 2:30pm – 5:30pm on Sunday. Hours are extended during Jun – Sep. Note: Access to St Sernin's tomb is allowed on November 29.

🌐 Canal du Midi

Created and built by Pierre-Paul Riquet, this 360 km long network of navigable waterway linking the Atlantic Ocean to the Mediterranean Sea is a UNESCO World Heritage Site since 1996.

TOULOUSE TRAVEL GUIDE

The idea germinated in 1500s when Francois I brought Leonardo Da Vinci to France. The plan was to link the Garonne and Aude rivers thus linking the Atlantic Ocean to the Mediterranean Sea. This would create a shortcut for the French ships as well as make it possible to avoid the hostile Spanish coastline.

The work was commissioned by Louis XIV in 1666. Chevalier de Clerville joined hands with Riquet to design the canal that was to have 328 different structures along its path. Work started with the western section till the eastern section was sanctioned in 1669. Riquet almost completed the work before his death 12 years later in 1681.

The project was completed at a cost of near 15 million livres, over 4 times the original budget. Work had started with 2000 workers, and at a point reached 12000. Women laborers were brought as there was a shortage of male workers. The canal, regarded as an engineering marvel in those times became a French symbol of power in the 17th century. The Saint Ferreol earthen dam built in 1675 on the Laudot River as a part of this project stood at a height of 115m and remained the highest dam in the world for over 150 years.

With 42000 trees from the 1830s stabilizing and decorating the banks of the Cana du Midi, it has become one the most popular waterways in Europe. The waterways, which were used to transfer mail and ferry passengers, are now used for pleasure activities like fishing, boating, and canoeing. The banks are ideal for cycling and there is a long stretch of covered bicycle path.

The Maison de la Haute-Garonne on the Autoroute A61 has free instructive exhibits on the Canal du Midi. The Musee ET Jardins du Canal du Midi, www.museecanaldumidi.fr, is a museum at Saint Ferreol dam dedicated to the dam and its creator Riquet. The 8600 sq feet museum has 6 thematic rooms highlighting the construction of the dam through models, audio-visuals and documents.

🌍 Cite de l'Espace (Science Museum)

Avenue Jean Gonord

31200 Toulouse

Tel: +33567 22 23 24

www.cite-espace.com/

Located to the east of Toulouse this space-based theme

park attracts the young and elderly alike. The park, opened in 1997 spreads over 9 acres and houses 2 planetariums (the new 280-seater planetarium is called the Stellarium), an IMAX theatre, and multiple exhibits. Within 3 years, the park attracted over a million visitors.

There is an exact replica of the Russian MIR Space Station There is a replica of the Russian Soyuz spacecraft, the most long lasting Russian spacecraft to date clocking over 50 years. There is a 53m tall model of Ariane 5 rocket, the European space launcher.

The usual park hours are from 9:30am – 5:00pm but the hours are extended to 7:00pm and 11:00pm on certain days. Ticket prices are: Adult – € 23.00; Children of 5 – 15 years – € 16.50. There are discounted tickets for disabled persons, jobseekers, and students.

There is a 10% discount with the Pass tourisme.

🌐 Saint Etienne Cathedral

Place Saint Etienne

31000 Toulouse

Location: Centre / Capitole

http://cathedrale.toulouse.free.fr/

The Cathedral Saint-Etienne de Toulouse or the Toulouse Cathedral is the seat of the archbishop of Toulouse and is a reminder of the grandeur of Gothic art of the medieval European period. The cathedral, made up of 2 churches, was built between the 12th and the 16th century.

As there were significant changes in the style of architecture during this period, the Toulouse Cathedral reflected the different styles in its design. The entrance to the Raymondine nave is of southern Gothic style, clearly different from the other part which is of the northern Gothic style. There is also a tower which has a Romanesque foundation but with Gothic style in certain parts.

The most interesting part of this piece of architecture is that one can easily demarcate the 2 primary styles of architecture. The aisles along with the exterior and interior look oddly different and disproportionate. There is a round pillar which almost stands as a demarcating line between the 2 styles.

The newer Northern Gothic style focused on grandeur to rival other cathedrals of the period, this dwarfing the nave that was built in the southern Gothic style.

The cathedral has a beautiful Rose Window, the design having a striking similarity with the ones in the Notre-Dame in Paris. There are 15 chapels with the oldest dating back to the late 13th century. Another notable feature of the cathedral is the beautiful stained glass.

There is a grand organ suspended 17m up that was restored by the famous Cavaille-Coll in 1868 and is still used during concerts. The cathedral also has a collection of ornamental elements, paintings, and tapestries.

Close to the Francois Verdier station, the Cathedral has free entry.

🌍 Airbus Factory Visit

Rue Franz Joseph Strauss

TOULOUSE TRAVEL GUIDE

31700 Blagnac

Tel: +3353 4394200

http://www.manatour.fr

Toulouse is one of the major seats of the global aviation industry with the global giant Airbus having its office and an assembly line in Blagnac. Airbus has 3 tours open to the public – Visit Airbus A380 Tour, Visit Airbus Panoramic Tour, and the Visit Airbus Green Tour. Each tour is of 90 minutes.

The most popular is the Airbus A380 Tour that takes a visitor through an audio-visual tour of the making of the aircraft. It also includes a view of the assembly line at the J L Lagerdere plant where an A380 aircraft is being assembled. For the aviation enthusiast it is a chance to see the assembly of the world's largest passenger

aircraft.

The Panoramic Tour is a 25 km bus ride through the 700

hectares of Airbus sites in Toulouse, with a view of the

SAS Headquarters and the pilot training centre.

The Green Tour is a bus ride educating and informing the

visitors about the eco-efficient solutions of Airbus to

reduce pollution and save energy and resources in the

aeronautical industry.

Although the tour is aimed at both adults and children, it

should be noted that the tour is in Blagnac and the whole

trip, including the journey, the waiting, and the tour can

take more than half a day. Tourists on a short visit to

TOULOUSE TRAVEL GUIDE

Toulouse should only go for this tour if one has special interest in aircrafts and aviation.

Prior reservation is required to attend the tour. For non-EU citizens, the booking must be done at least 2 days in advance. A photo ID is a must to gain entry; non-EU citizens should carry the passport. Group booking of 10 or more people require a deposit which is adjusted with the ticket price.

The Tours are open 6 days a week, except Sundays and bank holidays. A reserved slot is given to every visitor when the booking is done. It is preferable to reach before time so as to not miss the tour bus.

The tickets prices are: Adult – € 15 for A380 Tour and € 13 for the Panoramic and Green Tours. For a child, unemployed, or disabled person – € 13 for the A380 Tour, and € 11 for the other two tours. Free for children under the age of 6.

Musee des Augustins

21 Rue de Metz

31000 Toulouse

Location: Centre / Capitole

Tel: 0561 222182

http://www.augustins.org/

Surrounding a beautiful courtyard garden, the Musee des Augustins de Toulouse or the Augustin Museum is one of the oldest in France. It was opened to the public in 1795, shortly after the opening of the Louvre Museum in Paris. The museum has a rich collection of fine arts and architecture dating back to the Middle Ages.

The brick building housing the museum was originally a convent in the early 14th century. The hermits of St Augustin were allowed by Pope Clement V to build the convent as they were living there for almost a century. The construction of the St Augustins church that started in 1309 was completed in the beginning of the 16th century.

Vaults were added to the building in the later centuries. The spire and upper floors of the church were destroyed by lightning in 1550 and were never rebuilt. By the late 17th century there was a decline in the number of monks in the convent, the number dropped to around 30 in 1680.

This did not stop expansions and restorations of parts of the church and convent. The 17th century saw the addition of a large dormitory, a calefactoria, and a meditation room.

Although the convent was declared an 'Asset of the Nation' in 1789, part of the refractory was turned to stables after it was sold to Citizen Verdier. Art lovers started putting pressure on the preservation of the arts as those were exposed to wartime pillaging. The borough council soon made way to the opening of the Provincial Museum of the South of the Republic in the premises, paving the way for the Augustins Museum in later years. Several restorations were made to accommodate the works of art as well as the School Of Arts, that moved into the east and west wing in 1804.

It is interesting to note that although the museum was opened to protect the arts from getting destroyed, the building, a wonderful Gothic piece of architecture in itself, lost some of its sheen in the process.

The stained glass that adorned the windows, including the rose window, was destroyed to allow more light to view the exhibits. Walls were torn down to make way for galleries. The commissioning of the Temple of the Arts in the premise in 1831 resulted in the destruction of the paving and closing of the side chapels to make way for the Neo-classical style. Restyling and expansion carried on till the early 20th century.

In 1941 it was decided to restore the church and museum to restore some of its lost glory. A courtyard garden was created and galleries restored. Even stained glass was put at the Darcy staircase.

TOULOUSE TRAVEL GUIDE

Today the museum exhibits sculptures from the Romanesque, Gothic, and Renaissance period. There are also exhibits from the 17th to the 20th century when there was a heavy influence of the bourgeoisie. The collection of paintings from the renaissance period of French and Italian history includes some unique work like The Hunt by Giovanni.

The museum has a digital library of documents dating back to the late 18th century. There is also a photo library that is available online, and requests for photos can be either mailed or faxed to the museum office.

The museum is open daily morning from 10:00 am to 6:00 pm with late closings on Wednesdays (at 9:00 pm). It closes at 5:00 pm on 24th and 31st Dec and remains closed on 1st Jan, 1st May, and 25th Dec.

Ticket prices are: Adult – € 4. It is reduced to € 2 for groups of 15 or more. There is free entry to the permanent exhibits on the 1st Sunday of every month. Guided tours and workshops are also conducted at a nominal rate.

Musee Saint Raymond

1 Ter Place Saint-Sernin

31000 Toulouse

Location: Centre / Capitole

Tel: 0561 223144

www.saintraymond.toulouse.fr

The museum, dedicated to the life of the Celts and Romans in the Toulouse region, has over 1000 pieces of archaeological exhibits. It was declared a historic monument in 1975. The museum undertakes excavation work and offers great insights on the life and society of the Romans through the excavated objects.

The sites and monuments that are maintained by the museum include the Roman Amphitheater of Toulouse-Purpan and the Ancely Pool baths, the Funerary Basilica of Saint Pierre Des Cuisines, and the Basilica of St Sernin. Visitors are allowed entry to the amphitheater and the funerary basilica for an entrance fee of € 3.

Excavation works during as recent as 1994 to 1996 below the museum unearthed a Christian necropolis – cemetery with large tombstones. The necropolis had nearly a 100 lime kiln sepulchers or vaults and tombs. These can be viewed by visitors in the basement of the museum.

TOULOUSE TRAVEL GUIDE

The first floor displays works from the Martens-Tolosane village, 60 km south west of Toulouse. There are sculptures dating back to the late 3rd century. The exhibit of the busts of all the Roman leaders, lined up according to their reign is very popular. This collection of busts of Roman leaders is second to only the Louvre Museum in France.

The second floor has collections from the Roman town of Tolosa which includes some Gallic jewelry, household items in wood and stone, and statues.

An agreement between the state and the City of Toulouse allows the museum to preserve excavated objects. This made it possible for the museum to keep and study many objects that were excavated at the Capitole Metro Station.

TOULOUSE TRAVEL GUIDE

The museum has had a steady flow of visitors as it is one of the few museums where one can touch the exhibits and enjoy a number of interactive activities. There are so many items in the possession of the museum that not all can be displayed.

Special themed exhibitions are held from time to time to exhibit these reserved items. It is a good idea to use the audio guide for € 2 as there is such a wide variety of items in the museum. The museum also holds a number of events like film festivals on archeology, conferences, workshops and tours for the children and adults.

Ticket prices are: Adult – € 4; discounted tickets are available for children.

🌐 Hotel d'Assezat

Place d'Assezat

31000 Toulouse

Location: Centre / Capitole

Tel: 0561 120689

http://www.fondation-bemberg.fr/

This 17th century town mansion was built by Nicolas Bachelier for the merchant Pierre d'Assezat, by whose name the building is known today. Pierre d'Assezat made a huge fortune from woad, the plant used in dyeing, and responsible for the resurrection of Toulouse's economic fortunes around the 17th century.

Pierre himself was not able to see the completion of this building that was heavily inspired by the Renaissance palatial architecture. The construction started in 1555 and was continuing when Pierre died 26 years later. There is a lot of brickwork as is typical to many buildings in Toulouse. The townhouse has a big courtyard influenced by Italian mannerism and classicism.

The building was taken over by the City of Toulouse and now houses a major art gallery – the Bemberg Foundation. The art gallery exhibits the private collections of the tycoon Georges Bemberg. It has 14 rooms with 14 themes that include paintings, sculptures, books, and furniture.

Entry is free; however rentals are available for guided tours of the private collections.

 Pont Neuf

12 Place du Pont Neuf

TOULOUSE TRAVEL GUIDE

31000 Toulouse

The Pont Neuf or the 'new bridge' is the oldest surviving bridge on the Garonne River. It is also known as the Pont de Pierre and the Grand Pont. Construction of this 220m long bridge started in 1154 and was completed in 1632. However it took another 27 years to inaugurate the bridge in 1659. This arch bridge made of stone has 7 arches but not all the arches are in symmetry.

The bridge is very close to the old city attractions and is especially beautiful during sunset and nigh time when the lights come on, creating colorful reflections.

Budget Tips

Accommodation

Hotel Saint Severin

69 Rue Bayard

31000 Toulouse

Location: Near Train Station

Tel: 0561 627139

www.hotel-saint-severin.com

Located near the Marengo SNCF, the Saint Severin Hotel has a typical Toulouse style décor. It is also close to the metro and shuttle service. The hotel has a 24 hr service and has all the basic amenities including satellite TV, Wi-Fi, and direct telephone lines.

Single rooms start from € 48 and double rooms from € 56.

Breakfast can be taken in the room or the dining room and costs € 6.

Royal Wilson Hotel

6 Rue Labéda

31000 Toulouse

Location: Centre / Capitole

Tel: 05 61 124141

www.hotelroyalwilson-toulouse.com

The Royal Wilson Hotel is located at the heart of the old city centre, about half a km from the Capitole. It is close to the Jean Jaures and Capitole Metro station. It is 5 min from the TGV Matabiau train station.

The hotel has 27 air-con rooms with Wi-Fi, satellite TV and Internet access. Pets are allowed in the hotel. The hotel also has a private parking garage for its guests.

Room rates start from € 59 for a single or double room. Breakfast starts from € 8.50.

Hotel du Taur

2 Rue du Taur

31000 Toulouse

Location: Centre / Capitole

Tel: 0561 211754

www.hotel-du-taur.com

The hotel is located at the corner of the Capitole Square and Rue du Taur. It is close to the Capitole metro station.

The hotel has a 24/7 service with a multilingual reception staff. Parking is available next door at € 9 per day.

All 39 rooms are equipped with the basic amenities.

Room rates start from € 45 for single and double rooms.

Hotel Albert 1er (1st)

8 Rue Rivals

31000 Toulouse

Location: Centre / Capitole

Tel: 0561 211791

http://www.hotel-albert1.com/

Hotel Albert 1er has been operating since 1954 and is only a few hundred meters from the Capitole. It has won the European Ecolabel Award since 2012 for being environment friendly.

All the 47 rooms are non – smoking and have satellite TV with international channels, mini bar and a safe. The room rates start from € 55 for single room and € 59 for double rooms. Breakfast at the hotel costs € 11.

Hotel Excelsior

82 Rue Pierre Paul Riquet

31000 Toulouse

Location: Centre / Capitole

Tel: 0561 627125

www.excelsior-toulousecentre.com

Close to Jean-Juares station, the Excelsior Hotel is a no frills hotel. Basic room rate starts from € 29. For the rooms that have shower and toilet, the rate starts from € 40. Airport shuttle is available.

🌐 Restaurants, Cafés & Bars

L'Entrepotes

8 Rue des Blanchers

31000 Toulouse

Tel: 0561 227825

http://www.lentrepotestoulouse.fr/index.html

Owned and run by the husband and wife team of Franck

and Valery Sessa, this small cozy food place is ranked

highly by visitors and locals alike. It is closed on Sunday,

Monday, and Saturday lunch. The menu has a variety of

beef, veal, and duck, which is regarded a local specialty.

Main dishes start from about € 7.

Bapz Bakery and Tea Room

13, rue de la bourse,

31000 Toulouse, France (Saint Rome)

0561230663

http://www.bapz.fr/accueil.html

Located close to Pont Neuf, this British style café serves delicious pies, salads, and brunch specials. A 5 every evening homemade pastry is served. There is a lunch special at € 17. The friendly service along with the beautifully displayed cakes and tarts is a crowd favorite.

La Petit Rajasthan

1 Bis Rue Jules Chalande,

31000 Toulouse

Tel: 0561 237734

http://lepetitrajasthan.com/

Quite friendly to the pocket unlike many Indian restaurants, the la Petit Rajasthan restaurant has won wonderful reviews for its friendly staff and delicious food. It has only 30 covers so it would be good to reserve a place during weekends and holidays. A € 16.90 set menu gets you a three course meal along with rice, raita, starter, and a dessert.

Emile Restaurant

13 Place Saint-Georges

31000 Toulouse

Tel: 0561 210556

http://www.restaurant-emile.com/

Opened in the 1940s as a guesthouse, it was transformed to a restaurant in the 1960s. Housed in a Toulousaine brick house, the restaurant carries an old world charm in its décor and ambience. There is a local specialty menu available only from October to April. The restaurant also has a seafood menu (€ 40) and a menu of the day (€ 20). It also has a la carte menu. The restaurant serves a wide variety of wines.

Soup 'Here

25 Rue Pharaon

31000 Toulouse

Location: Centre / Capitole

Tel: 0954 464313

Located near the Place du Palais this small eatery serves soup and salads with a perfect pricing for budget travelers. The a la carte menu is from € 4–17. Lunch and evening menu start from € 9

 Shopping

Espace Graine de pastel

4 Place Saint Etienne

31000 Toulouse

Location: Centre / Capitole

Mobile: 0643 653100

www.grainedepastel.com

Located near the Farncois Verdier metro station, the shop specializes in products made with the extract of woad or blue pastel. Toulouse was known for the blue trade in the 16th and 17th century which made it a land of fortune. The Graine de pastel sells a number of cosmetic products ranging from soaps, lotions, body oils to organic cotton bath towels. Prices start from around € 7 for these organic products.

La Maison de la Violette

Face au 2 Boulevard Bonrepos

31000 Toulouse

Location: Near Train Station

Tel: 0561 990130

www.lamaisondelaviolette.fr

Located near the Marengo SNCF, this is a barge on the Canal du Midi. The beautiful wooden interior is dedicated to the color and fragrance of the violet flower. It was opened in 2000 by Helen Vie and sells sweets and perfumes related to the flower.

There is Foie gras with sweet and sour violet, Madeleines cranberry scented violets, and even apple salad violets to choose from. One can also shop online from their website. It is open from Monday to Saturday from 9:30 am to 12:30 pm and from 2:00 pm to 7:00 pm.

Marche des Carmes

Place des Carmes

31000 Toulouse

http://www.xn--march-des-carmes-fqb.com/index.html

This market selling fresh produce is open from Tuesday to Saturday from 7:00 to 12:30. One can get local delicacies like the cadanet bread, fresh French cheese, and locally made wine.

Nicolas Tourel

13 Rue Boulbonne

31000 Toulouse

Location: Centre / Capitole

Tel: 0561 524832

www.tourrel-joaillier.com

Nicolas Tourel is a twenty-year old family business of handcrafted jewelry. Nicolas Tourel was awarded the "Best Craftsman in France as Jeweler" in 2004. The store is open from Tuesday to Saturday from 10:30 am – 1:00 pm and from 2:00 pm – 6:30 pm. It is located near the Esquirol metro station.

Midica

13, place Esquirol,

31000 Toulouse

Tel: 0561 48282

http://www.midica.fr/

TOULOUSE TRAVEL GUIDE

This multipurpose shopping arcade stores a wide variety

of products. One can find from household items to

pharmacy items in this multi-storied arcade.

Know Before You Go

 Entry Requirements

By virtue of the Schengen agreement, visitors from other countries in the European Union will not need a visa when visiting France. Additionally Swiss visitors are also exempt. Visitors from certain other countries such as Andorra, Canada, the United Kingdom, Ireland, the Bahamas, Australia, the USA, Chile, Costa Rica, Croatia, El Salvador, Guatemala, Honduras, Israel, Malaysia, Mauritius, Monaco, Nicaragua, New Zealand, Panama, Paraguay, Saint Kitts and Nevis, San Marino, the Holy See, Seychelles, Taiwan and Japan do not need visas for a stay of less than 90 days. Visitors to France must be in possession of a valid passport that expires no sooner than three months after the intended stay. UK citizens will not need a visa to enter France. Visitors must provide proof of residence, financial support and the reason for their visit. If you wish to work or study in France, however, you will need a visa.

🌎 Health Insurance

Citizens of other EU countries are covered for emergency health care in France. UK residents, as well as visitors from Switzerland are covered by the European Health Insurance Card (EHIC), which can be applied for free of charge. Visitors from non-Schengen countries will need to show proof of private health insurance that is valid for the duration of their stay in France (that offers at least €37,500 coverage), as part of their visa application. A letter of coverage will need to be submitted to the French Embassy along with your visa application. American travellers will need to check whether their regular medical insurance covers international travel. No special vaccinations are required.

🌎 Travelling with Pets

France participates in the Pet Travel Scheme (PETS) which allows UK residents to travel with their pets without requiring quarantine upon re-entry. Certain conditions will need to be met. The animal will have to be microchipped and up to date on rabies vaccinations. In the case of dogs, France also requires vaccination against distemper. If travelling from another EU member country, you will need an EU pet passport. Regardless of the country, a Declaration of Non-Commercial Transport must be signed stating that you do not intend to sell your pet.

A popular form of travel with pets between the UK and France is via the Eurotunnel, which has special facilities for owners travelling with pets. This includes dedicated pet exercise areas and complimentary dog waste bags. Transport of a pet via this medium costs €24. The Calais Terminal has a special Pet Reception Building. Pets travelling from the USA will need to be at least 12 weeks old and up to date on rabies vaccinations. Microchipping or some form of identification tattoo will also be required. If travelling from another country, do inquire about the specific entry requirements for your pet into France and also about re-entry requirements in your own country.

🌐 Airports

There are three airports near Paris where most international visitors arrive. The largest of these is **Charles De Gaulle** (CDG) airport, which serves as an important hub for both international and domestic carriers. It is located about 30km outside Paris and is well-connected to the city's rail network. Most trans-Atlantic flights arrive here. **Orly** (ORY) is the second largest and oldest airport serving Paris. It is located 18km south of the city and is connected to several public transport options including a bus service, shuttle service and Metro rail. Most of its arrivals and departures are to other destinations within Europe. **Aéroport de Paris-Beauvais-Tillé** (BVA), which lies in Tillé near Beauvais, about 80km outside

Paris, is primarily used by Ryanair for its flights connecting Paris to Dublin, Shannon Glasgow and other cities.

There are several important regional airports. **Aéroport Nice Côte d'Azur** (NCE) is the 3rd busiest airport in France and serves as a gateway to the popular French Riviera. **Aéroport Lyon Saint-Exupéry** (LYS) lies 20km east of Lyon and serves as the main hub for connections to the French Alps and Provence. It is the 4th busiest airport of France. **Aéroport de Bordeaux** (BOD) served the region of Bordeaux. **Aéroport de Toulouse – Blagnac** (TLS), which lies 7km from Toulouse, provides access to the south-western part of France. **Aéroport de Strasbourg** (SXB), which lies 10km west of Strasbourg, served as a connection to Orly, Paris and Nice. **Aéroport de Marseille Provence** (MRS) is located in the town of Marignane, about 27km from Marseille and provides access to Provence and the French Riviera. **Aéroport Nantes Atlantique** (NTE) lies in Bouguenais, 8km from Nantes carriers and provides a gateway to the regions of Normandy and Brittany in the western part of France. **Aéroport de Lille** (LIL) is located near Lesquin and provides connections to the northern part of France.

 Airlines

Air France is the national flag carrier of France and in 2003, it merged with KLM. The airline has a Flying Blue rewards program, which allows members to earn, accumulate and redeem Flying Blue Miles on any flights with Air France, KLM or any other Sky Team airline. This includes Aeroflot, Aerolineas Argentinas, AeroMexico, Air Europa, Alitalia, China Airlines, China Eastern, China Southern, Czech Airlines, Delta, Garuda Indonesia, Kenya Airways, Korean Air, Middle Eastern Airlines, Saudia, Tarom, Vietnam Airlines and Xiamen Airlines.

Air France operates several subsidiaries, including the low-cost Transavia.com France, Cityjet and Hop! It is also in partnership with Air Corsica. Other French airlines are Corsairfly and XL Airways France (formerly Star Airlines).

France's largest intercontinental airport, Charles de Gaulle serves as a hub for Air France, as well as its regional subsidiary, HOP!. It also functions as a European hub for Delta Airlines. Orly Airport, also in Paris, serves as the main hub for Air France's low cost subsidiary, Transavia, with 40 different destinations, including London, Madrid, Copenhagen, Moscow, Casablanca, Algiers, Amsterdam, Istanbul, Venice, Rome, Berlin and Athens. Aéroport de Marseille Provence (MRS) outside Marseille serves as a hub to the region for budget airlines such as EasyJet and Ryanair. Aéroport Nantes Atlantique serves as a French base for the Spanish budget airline, Volotea.

 Currency

France's currency is the Euro. It is issued in notes in denominations of €500, €200, €100, €50, €20, €10 and €5. Coins are issued in €2, €1, 50c, 20c, 10c, 5c, 2c and 1c.

Banking & ATMs

If your ATM card is compatible with the MasterCard/Cirrus or Visa/Plus networks and configured for a 4-digit PIN, you will have no problem drawing money in France. Most French ATMs have an English language option. Remember to inform your bank of your travel plans before you leave. Keep an eye open around French ATMs to avoid pickpockets or scammers.

Credit Cards

Credit cards are frequently used throughout France, not just in shops, but also to pay for metro tickets, parking tickets, and motorway tolls and even to make phone calls at phone booths. MasterCard and Visa are accepted by most vendors. American Express and Diners Club are also accepted by the more tourist oriented businesses. Credit cards issued in Europe are smart cards that that are fitted with a microchip and require a PIN for each transaction. This means that a few ticket machines, self-service vendors and other businesses may not be configured to accept the older magnetic strip credit cards.

🌐 Tourist Taxes

All visitors to France pay a compulsory city tax or tourist tax ("taxe de séjour"), which is payable at your accommodation. Children are exempt from tourist tax. The rate depends on the standard of accommodation, starting with €0.75 per night for cheaper establishments going up to €4, for the priciest options. Rates are, of course, subject to change.

🌐 Reclaiming VAT

If you are not from the European Union, you can claim back VAT (or Value Added Tax) paid on your purchases in France. The VAT rate in France is 20 percent on most goods, but restaurant goods, food, transport and medicine are charged at lower rates. VAT can be claimed back on purchases of over €175 from the same shop, provided that your stay in France does not exceed six months. Look for shops that display a "Tax Free" sign. The shop assistant must fill out a form for reclaiming VAT. When you submit it at the airport, you can expect your refund to be debited within 30 to 90 days to your credit card or bank account. It can also be sent by cheque.

🌐 Tipping Policy

In French restaurants, a 15 percent service charge is added directly to your bill and itemized with the words *service compris* or "tip included". This is a legal requirement for taxation purposes. If the service was unusually good, a little extra will be appreciated. In an expensive restaurant where there is a coat check, you may add €1 per coat. In a few other situations, a tip will be appreciated. You can give an usherette in a theatre 50 cents to €1, give a porter €1 per bag for helping with your luggage or show your appreciation for a taxi driver with 5-10 percent over the fare. It is also customary to tip a hair dresser or a tour guide 10 percent.

🌐 Mobile Phones

Most EU countries, including France uses the GSM mobile service. This means that most UK phones and some US and Canadian phones and mobile devices will work in France. While you could check with your service provider about coverage before you leave, using your own service in roaming mode will involve additional costs. The alternative is to purchase a French SIM card to use during your stay in France. France has four mobile networks. They are Orange, SFR, Bouygues Telecom and Free. In France, foreigners are barred from applying for regular phone contract and the data rates are somewhat pricier on pre-paid phone services than in most European countries. You will need to show some form of identification, such as a passport when you make your purchase and it can take up to 48 hours to activate a French SIM card. If there is an Orange Boutique nearby, you can buy a SIM for €3.90. Otherwise, the Orange Holiday package is available for €39.99. Orange also sells a 4G device which enables your own portable Wi-Fi hotspot for €54.90. SFR offers a SIM card, simply known as le card for €9.99. Data rates begin at €5 for 20Mb.

🌐 Dialling Code

The international dialling code for France is +33.

🌐 Emergency Numbers

All emergencies: (by mobile) 112
Police: 17
Medical Assistance: 15
Fire and Accidents: 18
SOS All Emergencies (hearing assisted: 114)
Visa: 0800 90 11 79
MasterCard: 0800 90 13 87
American Express: 0800 83 28 20

Public Holidays

1 January: New Year's Day (Nouvel an / Jour de l'an / Premier de l'an)

March - April: Easter Monday (Lundi de Pâques)

1 May: Labor Day (Fête du Travail / Fête des Travailleurs)

8 May: Victory in Europe Day (Fête de la Victoire)

May: Ascension Day (Ascension)

May: Whit Monday (Lundi de Pentecôte)

14 July: Bastille Day (Fête nationale)

15 August: Assumption of Mary (L'Assomption de Marie)

1 November: All Saints Day (La Toussaint)

11 November: Armistace Day (Armistice de 1918)

25 December: Christmas Day (Noël)

Good Friday and St Stephens Day (26 December) are observed only in Alsace and Moselle.

🌍 Time Zone

France falls in the Central European Time Zone. This can be calculated as Greenwich Mean Time/Co-ordinated Universal Time (GMT/UTC) +2; Eastern Standard Time (North America) -6; Pacific Standard Time (North America) -9.

🌍 Daylight Savings Time

Clocks are set forward one hour on the last Sunday of March and set back one hour on the last Sunday of October for Daylight Savings Time.

🌐 School Holidays

The academic year in France is from the beginning of September to the end of June. The long summer holiday is from the beginning of July to the end of August. There are three shorter vacation periods. All schools break up for a two week break around Christmas and New Year. There are also two week breaks in February and April, but this varies per region, as French schools are divided into three zones, which take their winter and spring vacations at different times.

🌐 Driving Laws

The French drive on the ride hand side of the road. If you have a non-European driving licence, you will be able to use it in France, provided that the licence is valid and was issued in your country of residence before the date of your visa application. There are a few other provisions. The minimum driving age in France is 18. Your licence will need to be in French or alternately, you must carry a French translation of your driving permit with you.

In France, the speed limit depends on weather conditions. In dry weather, the speed limit is 130km per hour for highways, 110km per hour for 4-lane expressways and 90km per hour for 2 or 3-lane rural roads. In rainy weather, this is reduced to 110km, 100km and 80km per hour respectively. In foggy weather with poor visibility, the speed limit is 50km per hour on all roads. On urban roads, the speed limit is also 50km per hour.

By law, French drivers are obliged to carry a breathalyser in their vehicle, but these are available from most supermarkets, chemists and garages for €1. The legal limit is 0.05, but for new drivers who have had their licence for less than three years, it is 0.02. French motorways are called autorouts. It is illegal in France to use a mobile phone while driving, even if you have a headset.

🌍 Drinking Laws

The legal drinking age in France is 18. The drinking policy regarding public spaces will seem confusing to outsiders. Each municipal area imposes its own laws. In Paris, alcohol consumption is only permitted in licensed establishments. It is strictly forbidden in parks and public gardens.

🌍 Smoking Laws

From 2007, smoking has been banned in indoor spaces such as schools, government buildings, airports, offices and factories in France. The ban was extended in 2008 to hospitality venues such as restaurants, bars, cafes and casinos. French trains have been smoke free since December 2004.

🌍 Electricity

Electricity: 220-240 volts

Frequency: 50 Hz

Electricity sockets in France are unlike those of any other country. They are hermaphroditic, meaning that they come equipped with both prongs and indents. When visiting from the UK, Ireland, the USA or even another European country, you will need a special type of adaptor to accommodate this. If travelling from the USA, you will also need a converter or step-down transformer to convert the current to to 110 volts, to avoid damage to your appliances. The latest models of many laptops, camcorders, mobile phones and digital cameras are dual-voltage with a built in converter.

🌍 Food & Drink

France is a paradise for dedicated food lovers and the country has a vast variety of well-known signature dishes. These include foie gras, bouillabaisse, escargots de Bourgogne, Coq au vin, Bœuf Bourguignon, quiche Lorraine and ratatouille. A great budget option is crêpes or pancakes. Favorite sweets and pastries include éclairs, macarons, mille-feuilles, crème brûlée and croissants.

The country is home to several world-famous wine-growing regions, including Alsace, Bordeaux, Bourgogne, Champagne,

Corse, Côtes du Rhône, Languedoc-Roussillon, Loire, Provence and Sud-Ouest and correctly matching food to complimentary wine choices is practically a science. Therein lies the key to enjoying wine as the French do. It accompanies the meal. Drinking wine when it is not lunch or dinner time is sure to mark you as a foreigner. Pastis and dry vermouth are popular aperitifs and favorite after-dinner digestifs include cognac, Armagnac, calvados and eaux de vie. The most popular French beer is Kronenbourg, which originates from a brewery that dates back to 1664.

Websites

http://www.rendezvousenfrance.com/

http://www.france.com/

http://www.francethisway.com/

http://www.france-voyage.com/en/

http://www.francewanderer.com/

http://wikitravel.org/en/France

http://www.bonjourlafrance.com/index.aspx

Made in the USA
Las Vegas, NV
23 April 2023

70967405R00044